Contents

Scholastic BookFiles™

A READING GUIDE TO

The Giver

by Lois Lowry

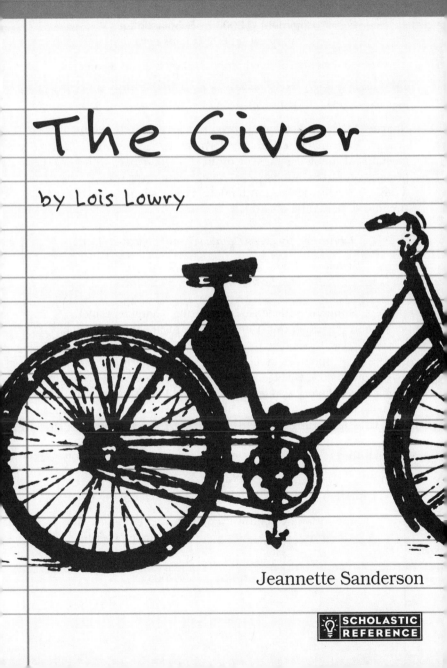

Jeannette Sanderson

SCHOLASTIC
REFERENCE

Library of Congress Cataloging-in-Publication Data

Scholastic BookFiles: A Reading Guide to The Giver
by Lois Lowry/Jeannette Sanderson.
p. cm.
Summary: Discusses the writing, characters, plot,
and themes of this 1994 Newbery Award–winning book.
Includes discussion questions and activities.
Includes bibliographical references (p.).
1. Lowry, Lois. Giver—Juvenile literature.   2. Science fiction,
American—History and criticism—Juvenile literature.   [1. Lowry,
Lois. Giver.   2. American literature—History and criticism.]
I. Title: A Reading Guide to The Giver by Lois Lowry.   II. Title.
PS3562.O923 G5837   2003
813′.54—dc21   2002191233
0-439-46356-4

10 9 8 7 6 5 4 3 2 1   03 04 05 06 07

Composition by Brad Walrod/High Text Graphics, Inc.
Cover and interior design by Red Herring Design

Printed in the U.S.A.   23
First printing, July 2003

"From the time I was eight or nine, I wanted to be a writer. Writing was what I liked best in school; it was what I did best in school."

—Lois Lowry

Lois Lowry says that, aside from photography, she has never wanted to do anything but write. The author of more than twenty-five books for children and young adults, Lowry developed a love of language, and a love of stories, early on. "I was a solitary child," she remembers, "born the middle of three, who lived in the world of books and my own imagination. There are some children, and I was this kind of child, who are introverts and love to read—who prefer to curl up with a book than to hang out with friends or play at the ball field. Children like that begin to develop a feeling for language and for story. And that was true for me—that's how I became a writer."

Lois Lowry was born on March 20, 1937, to Katharine and Robert Hammersberg. Her sister, Helen, was three when Lois was born; her brother, Jon, was born six years after Lois.

Lowry's father was an army dentist, and his military career led the family all over the world. Lois was born in Honolulu, Hawaii, where she lived until she was three. Then the family moved to New York City for two years. When Robert Hammersberg was sent overseas during World War II, Lois, her mother, and her sister went to stay with her mother's parents at their home in Carlisle, Pennsylvania. That's where her brother was born. Seven years later, the family went to join her father in Tokyo, Japan, where he was stationed. They lived there for three years before returning to the United States and New York City, where Lowry went to high school.

After high school, Lowry went to Brown University in Providence, Rhode Island, but left after her sophomore year to get married. Since her husband was a naval officer, Lowry continued making the frequent moves required of military families. Over the next six years, she lived in California, Connecticut, Florida, South Carolina, and Massachusetts. In the early 1960s, with four children under the age of five, Lowry and her husband moved to Maine to raise their family.

"My children grew up in Maine," Lowry says. "So did I. I . . . finally began to write professionally, the thing I had dreamed of doing since those childhood years when I had endlessly scribbled stories and poems in notebooks."

Lowry went back to college in Maine. She got her degree from the University of Southern Maine in 1973, and went to graduate school. In 1976, she discovered her chosen career: writing for children. "Since childhood, I always wanted to be a writer," Lowry says. "I majored in writing in college, but I thought of myself as a writer for adults. It wasn't until I wrote my first book for kids in 1976 that I realized it was something that I loved doing. Now I hardly ever write for adults."

Lowry has written about many topics, some autobiographical, others not. Her first book, *A Summer to Die*, is about the death of an older sibling. She wrote the novel from personal experience: She lost her own sister to cancer in 1962. But whether or not the topics are based on her own experience, the feelings are. "Every time I write a book, I feel all the same feelings I felt when I was nine," Lowry has said.

While she may express the feelings of a nine-year-old in her writing, Lowry expresses the concerns of a grown woman. "I have grandchildren now," she says. "For them, I feel a greater urgency to do what I can to convey the knowledge that we live intertwined on this planet and that our future as human beings depends upon our caring more, and doing more, for one another."

Books, Lowry says, are one way to understand this interconnectedness. "The man that I named The Giver passed along to the boy knowledge, history, memories, color, pain, laughter, love, and truth. Every time you place a book in the hands of a child, you do the same thing. . . . Each time a child opens a book, he pushes open the gate that separates him from Elsewhere. It gives him choices, it gives him freedom."

Lowry sits at her desk every day, typing and retyping, putting together stories that open the gate to Elsewhere. "I have a relationship with—and an obligation to—the reader," she says, "because I affect that person's life and thinking, and that is no small responsibility."

In addition to doing the writing that she loves, Lowry finds time for a number of other activities. She is an avid reader. "Sitting around eating fresh apricots and reading a good book is my idea of heaven," Lowry says, adding that this was one of her favorite activities when she was ten, too. She also loves gardening—she has two houses with flower gardens—and cooking. She knits for her children and grandchildren, and likes to play bridge and go to the movies. And, she is an accomplished photographer; her work graces the covers of her books *The Giver, Number the Stars,* and *Gathering Blue.*

Lowry now lives in Cambridge, Massachusetts, and spends her weekends at a farmhouse in New Hampshire with a Tibetan terrier named Bandit.

"We can forget pain.... And it is comfortable to do so. But I also wonder...is it safe to do that, to forget?"

—Lois Lowry

L ois Lowry describes the origins of *The Giver* as a river that began back when she was eleven years old. At the time, her family lived in Tokyo, Japan, where her father was stationed after World War II. They lived in a small American community there. The way Lowry describes it, the fenced-off community shared some traits with the community in which Jonas lives: It was comfortable, familiar, and safe.

But, like Jonas after he begins receiving memories, Lowry did not want comfortable, familiar, and safe. Day after day, she rode her bicycle out of the gate that closed off her community. She would ride to an area of Tokyo called Shibuya. Lowry says she loved the feel of the place, "the vigor and the garish brightness and the noise: all such a contrast to my own life." For Lowry, Shibuya was Elsewhere. The river started there. As she grew, Lowry added more memories, thoughts, and ideas to this river.

She added memories from when she was a freshman in college and lived in a small dorm of fourteen young women. Thirteen of the women—Lowry included—were very much alike. They dressed alike, they acted alike. But the fourteenth woman was different. Lowry remembers that she and her roommates didn't "tease or torment" the woman who was different, but did "something worse": They ignored her, pretending that she didn't exist. "Somehow by shutting her out, we make ourselves feel comfortable. Familiar. Safe," Lowry says.

These memories, as well as the remorseful thoughts that followed, flowed into the river.

The river rose when Lowry was sent by a magazine editor to interview a painter who lived alone off the coast of Maine. She and the man talked a lot about color. "It is clear to me that although I am a highly visual person—a person who sees and appreciates form and composition and color—this man's capacity for seeing color goes far beyond mine," Lowry says. She adds that she wished "that he could have somehow magically given me the capacity to see the way he did."

Lowry photographed the man and kept a copy of the photograph, because there was something about his eyes that haunted her. (This photograph is now on the cover of *The Giver.*) The artist later went blind, though he said he could still see flowers in his memory. "Doesn't that make you think of The Giver?" Lowry asks.

Over the years, many more memories, thoughts, and ideas were added to the river. There was the time she heard of a crazed killer and felt relieved that he was not in her own neighborhood—then, moments later, felt ashamed to feel such relief. "How safe I deluded myself into feeling," she says, "by reducing my own realm of caring to my own familiar neighborhood."

Lowry's experiences with her elderly parents also added to the river that would become *The Giver*. "Both of my parents were dying when I wrote the book," Lowry says. "So the topic of memories and the transfer of memories from one generation to the next was very much on my mind."

Lowry says that though her mother was quite ill, "her mind was intact. She wanted to tell me the stories of her past . . . it was her life she wanted to pass along."

But her father was losing his memories. During one visit, he pointed to a picture of Lois's older sister, Helen, who had died of cancer when she was just twenty-eight years old. "That's Helen," he'd said. "I can't remember exactly what happened to her."

And Lowry thought, *We can forget pain. . . . And it is comfortable to do so. But . . . is it safe to do that, to forget?*

It was from this river of memories, thoughts, and ideas that Lois Lowry wrote *The Giver*.

About *The Giver*

◆ *Jonas is always careful about language, trying to choose just the right words. Is he like you in that regard? How important do you think it is to choose just the right words?*

Yes, Jonas is like me in valuing the precision of words. . . . (It's part of my job after all, to choose just the right words as I make my way through the writing of a book.) Though because of the world in which he lives, he has no feeling for the beauty of language, or the subtlety it can have.

◆ *What do you think is the most appealing aspect about the community in which Jonas lives? What is the least appealing?*

I like the safety and comfort of it: the absence of crime, poverty, deprivation, prejudice. But the lack of creativity and imagination is the most troubling aspect to me.

◆ The Giver *is one of the American Library Association's most frequently challenged books. What do you say to people who want to remove from library shelves a book that shows just how harmful lack of choice can be?*

I sometimes explain to kids, in particular, that people who challenge books do so because they care about children and their welfare. The irony, though, if you think it through, is that they make the world a more dangerous place by taking away freedom. The people who inhabited the world of *The Giver* had made their world very safe, very comfortable. But they had done it by taking away freedom. And there were no books left.

♦ *If a reader took away only one thing from this book, what would you want it to be?*

The thing I hope readers will learn from *The Giver* is the importance of having choice, and the importance of making good choices.

About being a writer

♦ *When do you write? Will you describe a typical day for us?*

I work at home, in a room that was once a doctor's office (this house once belonged to a doctor, and his office was attached to the house. I took away all his cabinets and created a wall of bookcases in their place). I go into my office every morning and I stay here all day, unless, of course, I'm traveling.

I sit here *[Lowry answered these interview questions from her office.]* at a MacIntosh computer and put words on a page. I am not always writing fiction—though there is always a book-in-progress in the computer. I have to spend a lot of time answering mail, doing interviews, writing speeches, etc. But the time with fiction is the time I love most. I write sentences, rewrite them, say them aloud, listen to their cadence, and write them again. I find ways to make them flow into the next sentences and paragraphs . . . to make the narrative move along smoothly; to make the characters seem real. Writing is a solitary occupation, of course, but, for me, never lonely. My head is so populated with my fictional people, and they become quite real to me.

♦ *How do you know when you're ready to begin writing a new book?*

I think about a book for a long time before I begin writing. It's only when the character comes alive in my imagination . . . when I know where in his story I will encounter him or her, in other words, where the book will begin. By then I know everything that has gone before. But I don't want to start too far back. The best stories begin in the middle of something. In *The Giver*, for example . . . I knew, before I began, what Jonas had been doing for eleven years. But I realized I needed to start on one particular day when he was almost twelve.

♦ *How important is reading to your writing?*

Reading is absolutely essential. You don't enjoy cooking if you've never eaten good food. And why would you write if you didn't read, and love reading? For a writer, reading is a constant education, as well. You learn from poor writers and you are inspired by great ones.

◆ *You've said that you don't read children's books by other authors. Why not?*

I find that the fiction I most enjoy is fiction in which I can relate to the main character...identify with him or her. That means that I most enjoy fiction about people my age, people who face problems that I have faced, or that I can imagine facing. Of course, having been a child...and because I have a good memory of my childhood...I can enjoy books for kids. But I have limited time for reading. So I spend it on adult books.

◆ *What's your favorite thing about being a writer? What's your least favorite?*

I like the solitude of it. I don't think I'd enjoy a job that required constant interaction with other people. Least favorite? The business end of it: contracts, copyrights, etc. Boooorring. But necessary, of course.

◆ *What do you find easiest when writing? What do you find hardest?*

Hmmmm. Have to think about that one. Easiest, I guess, is starting and ending. I always find the beginnings of manuscripts an exhilarating time. And I like (even though readers are always bugging me about the ending of *The Giver*) the conclusions of books: figuring out where, exactly, to end, so that everything important in the book is part of the ending....But at the same time, I don't want the ending to be too neatly tied up, because I want to leave the reader with things to think and wonder about.

And that leaves, as the hardest part, the middle. There is so much to weave in and through the middle. The mechanics of it are difficult at times.

◆ *You are a photographer as well as a writer. How does your photography inform your writing in general, and how did it inform your writing of* The Giver, *in particular? (Aside from the beautiful cover art.)*

As a photographer it is always a question of choosing film, lenses, focus, depth of field, etc. And the composition as well. The same things apply to writing: where to place things, how to focus in on the important things, what to blur. In addition, as a writer . . . I tend to SEE what I'm writing; I go about it very visually.

◆ *What advice do you have for children who would like to be writers? What do you suggest they write about?*

Read a lot, of course. And think about what you read. That's how you learn what makes stories work. Write for yourself, and to practice how to put things together on a page. Don't think for one second, ever, about "how can I get this published." Think, instead, about the beauty of the language: how it feels and flows, how you can make it say just what you want it to.

What should they write about? The things that trouble them. The things they fear. The things that bring them the most joy.

General

You've said you were painfully shy as a child. Are you still shy? How has your shyness influenced the stories you write?

Yes, I am [shy], but I have learned to conceal that fairly well and to make my way through the necessary public events that are part of my life now. I think being an introvert has made me introspective. I think a lot, instead of talking a lot. Thinking is a very important part of being a writer. And so is observation. I am a watcher of people. It serves me well as a writer.

If you weren't a writer, what might you be?

Well, I would enjoy being a filmmaker, I think. Or a designer of houses. Not an architect—I'm not interested in the engineering and structural stuff. But I love renovating old houses. Right now I'm in the middle of fixing up a house built in 1768. There are paint samples spread out all over my desk.

What's one thing, besides writing, that you're really good at? What's one thing that you're really bad at?

I'm a pretty good cook, and I like entertaining friends . . . that goes along with my love of fixing up houses. I'm a very low-level Martha Stewart type, I think.

And I am SOOOOOO bad at anything athletic. Bad skier. Terrible tennis player. I'm a good swimmer, though, so I'm not completely hopeless.

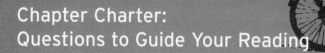
The following questions will help you think about the important parts of each chapter.

Chapter 1

- What do you imagine it means when someone is "released"?
- What are some clues that Jonas's community is different from the one in which you live?

Chapter 2

- How would you feel not to have your own individual birthday?
- If you were attending the Ceremony of Twelve with Jonas, what Assignment do you think the Elders would select for you?

Chapter 3

- How would you feel to be watched all the time, the way Jonas is?
- Do you think it says something about Jonas that he sees the apple change?

Chapter 4

- Jonas's community has a lot of rules. Do you think that's a good thing or a bad thing? Why?

Chapter 5

- Why was Jonas embarrassed about telling his dream?

- How important is sameness in Jonas's community? How important is it in your community?

Chapter 6

- All the members of Jonas's family had to sign a pledge that they would not become attached to the newchild, Gabe. Do you think it's possible to keep such a promise?
- What do you think of how families in Jonas's community are formed?

Chapter 7

- Do you think Asher should have been given the discipline wand when he was three, for saying "smack" instead of "snack"?
- How would you feel if you were in Jonas's shoes and the Chief Elder skipped right over you when she was making Assignments?

Chapter 8

- What do you think Jonas's Capacity to See Beyond is?
- Would you rather be selected, as Jonas was, or assigned, as his groupmates were?

Chapter 9

- Jonas tells himself several times that things can't change between him and his best friend, Asher. Do you think they can? Do you think they will?
- Why does Jonas find the final rule in his instructions, "You may lie," so unsettling?

Chapter 10

- What do you think it means to live in a place where no doors are ever locked?
- Jonas says, "I thought there was only us. I thought there was only now." Do you think that's a good way to live?

Chapter 11

- Can you imagine giving up such things as snow and hills because they are impractical?

Chapter 12

- Imagine a world without color. What color would you miss most?
- What value, if any, is there to Sameness?

Chapter 13

- Do you agree with Jonas that people have to be protected from wrong choices?
- As Jonas continues his training, he often finds himself angry with his groupmates and his family. Why?
- The Giver says that without memories, knowledge is meaningless. What does he mean?

Chapter 14

- Do you agree that painful memories are made easier when they are shared?
- Do you think it's fair that one person in the community—The Receiver—should have to be burdened and pained by memories so that no one else is?

Chapter 15

- Why do you think The Giver asks Jonas to forgive him?

Chapter 16

- The Giver gives Jonas many good memories. What are some of *your* best memories?
- Do you think the elderly should be part of the community, or separate, as in Jonas's community?
- Do you think Jonas's parents love him? Do you think they know what love is?
- Do you agree with Jonas that things could be different? How?

Chapter 17

- Why didn't the game of good guys and bad guys that Jonas's friends play seem harmless to Jonas anymore? Should Jonas have asked them to stop playing it? Why or why not?

Chapter 18

- Do you think Rosemary sounds like she was or wasn't brave?
- Why did The Giver seem distracted after telling Jonas to stay away from the river?

Chapter 19

- What do you think of what Jonas's community calls "release"? Were you surprised at what it was?
- How do you think this new knowledge will affect Jonas?

Chapter 20

- Jonas knows that if his plan fails, he could be killed. But he believes that if he stays, his life is no longer worth living. Do you agree?
- Do you think The Giver should go with Jonas or stay? Why?

Chapter 21

- How does Jonas show that he understands that the meaning of everything is to care about others?
- How do you think The Giver will feel when he realizes Jonas is gone? How will Jonas's friends and family feel?
- Why is the community so desperate to get Jonas back?

Chapter 22

- Jonas briefly wonders whether he made the wrong choice when he decided to run away. What do you think?

Chapter 23

- Although most of the memories have left Jonas, the feelings have not. Why do you think that is?
- How do you think the story ends?

> "'Jonas,' she said, speaking not to him
> alone but to the entire community of
> which he was a part, 'you will be
> trained to be our next Receiver of
> Memory. We thank you for your
> childhood.'"
>
> —Chief Elder, *The Giver*

The Giver is the story of a boy who lives in a seemingly perfect futuristic world and what he does when he learns the great price his community pays for such perfection.

The story starts with eleven-year-old Jonas worrying about the upcoming Ceremony of Twelve. This ceremony is when the Elevens are given their Assignments.

One evening before the Ceremony, Jonas's father, a Nurturer, brings home a newchild who needs extra nurturing. Jonas's father hopes to help the baby, named Gabe, grow and learn to sleep, so that the Committee will not vote to release him.

The Ceremony holiday finally arrives. The first day begins with the Naming of the newchildren. Gabe is not at the ceremony;

Jonas's father received permission from the Committee to allow the newchild an additional year to reach the proper milestones.

The Ceremony of Twelve begins the next day after lunch. The Chief Elder makes the Assignments, but skips Jonas when it is his turn. After she makes the final Assignment, the Chief Elder apologizes to Jonas. Then she says that he has been "selected to be our next Receiver of Memory." She says that the Committee failed in their last selection ten years ago, and has been very careful with this one. She explains that the job, the most honored in the community, requires that The Receiver be alone and apart, and that Jonas will need a tremendous amount of courage because he will be faced "with pain of a magnitude that none of us here can comprehend because it is beyond our experience." Jonas wonders if he has this courage.

The Chief Elder says that The Receiver must also have the Capacity to See Beyond. Jonas looks out at the crowd, and something happens to their faces—they change, the way an apple he had tossed with his friend had changed. He thinks that maybe he does have this quality.

That night, Jonas reads the rules and instructions for his Assignment. The last rule—you may lie—frightens him. "What if *others—adults*—had, upon becoming Twelves, received in their instructions the same terrifying sentence?" Did others lie?

Jonas begins his training the next day. The Receiver tells Jonas, "My job is to transmit to you all of the memories I have within me. Memories of the past. . . . Memories of the whole world."

Jonas is confused. "I thought there was only us. I thought there was only now." "There's much more," The Receiver tells him. "There's all that goes beyond—all that is Elsewhere—and all that goes back, and back, and back."

The current Receiver becomes The Giver and gives Jonas his first memory: that of a sled ride down a hill. When Jonas asks why snow, sleds, and hills no longer exist, The Giver explains that they became obsolete when the community decided to go to Sameness.

The next day, Jonas notices his friend Fiona's hair change, the way the apple and the faces in the crowd at the Ceremony had changed. Jonas asks The Giver about it. The Giver explains that Jonas is starting to see the color red. Jonas learns that there once were a lot of colors but that the community made the choice to do away with them to go to Sameness.

As he continues his training, Jonas feels frustrated to realize how few choices he has. He knows that it's safer this way, but it bothers him nonetheless.

Meanwhile, the newchild still isn't sleeping well, so Jonas tries taking him into his room at night. The first time Gabe fusses, Jonas rubs the baby's back. As he does so, he remembers a wonderful sail The Giver gave to him. The memory begins to fade, and Jonas realizes he is giving the memory to the baby. It helps Gabe sleep. Jonas does not tell The Giver that he has given away a memory.

The Giver gives Jonas many happy memories, but increasingly painful memories, too. Jonas begins to look at his family and groupmates differently. They have never seen color. They have never known pain. These thoughts make him feel very lonely. He asks The Giver why everyone can't have memories. "I think it would seem a little easier if the memories were shared," he says.

The Giver agrees. "But," he says, "then everyone would be burdened and pained. They don't want that. And that's the real reason The Receiver is so vital to them, and so honored. They selected me—and you—to lift that burden from themselves."

The Giver tells him that when The Receiver-in-training failed ten years ago, after only five weeks, the memories she had received were released, and everyone had access to them. "It was chaos," he says.

Jonas wonders aloud what would happen to the community if anything happened to him. He has been receiving memories for nearly a year. "If they lost *you*, with all the training you've had now, they'd have all those memories again themselves," The Giver says. "They wouldn't know how to deal with it at all."

"The only way *I* deal with it is by having you there to help me," Jonas says.

That gives The Giver an idea. "I suppose I could help the whole community the way I've helped you," he says. "It's an interesting concept. I need to think about it some more."

Jonas then tells The Giver that his father was going to release a newborn twin that morning. Jonas's concept of release is that the person is sent to Elsewhere. The Giver tells Jonas that he thinks he should watch the video of that release.

Jonas watches on the video screen as his father inserts a needle into a baby's forehead. He listens to his father's cheerful voice say, "All done. That wasn't so bad, was it?" He watches the baby die. His mind reels. "*He killed it! My father killed it!*"

Jonas refuses to go home that night. The Giver says he can spend the night with him. When Jonas rails against his father's actions, against all the people who perform releases, The Giver tells him, "They can't help it. *They know nothing.*" He explains that feelings are not part of the life they've learned, that he and Jonas are the only ones in the community who have feelings.

That evening, The Giver tells Jonas that "having you here with me over the past year has made me realize that things must change. . . . Now for the first time I think there might be a way." And they make a plan for The Giver to help Jonas to escape, so that the people will live with memories again.

Jonas wants The Giver to go with him, but his friend refuses. He says he must stay to help the community deal with the memories. "If you get away," The Giver tells Jonas, "if you get beyond, if you get to Elsewhere, it will mean that the community has to bear the burden themselves, of the memories you had been holding for them. I think they can, and that they will acquire some wisdom. But it will be desperately hard for them."

"Giver," Jonas says. "You and I don't need to *care* about the rest of them." But as soon as he says that, he is ashamed, because "of course they needed to care. It was the meaning of everything."

Jonas is sure the plan will work. But when he goes home, he learns that the Committee has decided to release Gabe the next morning. Jonas knows then that he has to flee right away, without The Giver's help.

In the middle of the night Jonas straps Gabe into the child seat on the back of his father's bicycle. Then he pedals away from the community, toward Elsewhere. Jonas's only regret is that he does not get to say good-bye to The Giver.

Jonas rides hard through the night, knowing that daylight will bring knowledge of his and Gabe's disappearance. At dawn he stops in an isolated field where he and Gabe eat and then sleep.

They go on like this for days, bicycling through the night, sleeping during the day. Jonas's greatest fear is the search planes. Whenever he hears them, he holds Gabe and hides.

One day the planes stop looking for them. The landscape changes, too. It is no longer flat and smooth. Now it is bumpy. Jonas feels "simple moments of exquisite happiness" when he sees wildflowers, birds, the wind shifting in the trees. But he is also very afraid now, afraid that he and Gabe will starve. He wonders briefly if, finally given a choice to make, he made the wrong one. Then, when he thinks of Gabe, he knows he had no choice. He had to flee.

Jonas and Gabe continue their journey, hungry and increasingly cold. Jonas feels certain that he is reaching his destination. They come to a place where it snows. He can no longer ride his bike. And it is so hard to walk. Jonas thinks of just lying down with the baby in the soft cold, of giving up. But he won't. He tries to call back some of the memories of warmth that The Giver had given to him, but they are weak. Those memories are almost all lost to him now, returned to the community.

Then, as he trudges up a snow-covered hill carrying the baby inside his tunic, he feels he knows what is waiting for him at the top. "We're almost there, Gabriel," he tells the baby. Somehow Jonas knows that a sled will be waiting at the top of the hill, and it is. Jonas climbs on and, holding tight to Gabriel, sets off down the hill. He sees lights in the distance. And, for the first time, he hears people singing.

Thinking about the plot

- In what ways did Jonas's world seem perfect?
- What were some of the things missing from Jonas's world?
- What are some of the reasons that Jonas felt he had to run away?

> "'I don't know what you mean when you say "the whole world" or "generations before him." I thought there was only us. I thought there was only now.'"
>
> —Jonas, *The Giver*

The Giver is a science-fiction novel that takes place in a "very different culture and time," Lowry says. The author establishes the book's unusual setting in a number of ways.

One way Lowry establishes the book's setting is by making Jonas's world one full of rules, some familiar, others totally strange. There are rules about keeping feelings hidden, about having more than two children—one male, one female—in each family unit, and about bragging, among other things. There are so many rules, in fact, that each household has the community's Book of Rules as one of the three books that it is allowed to—and required to—own.

Lowry also places readers in unfamiliar territory with the words she uses to describe things that are familiar to us. For instance, a family becomes a family unit, a home becomes a dwelling, and a stuffed animal becomes a comfort object.

In addition to making the familiar unfamiliar with her use of words, Lowry uses capitalization to remove the reader from any familiar time and place. The author capitalizes the names of important events and ceremonies, such as the Naming, when newchildren are given their names and the Ceremony of Twelve, when children are given their lifetime work Assignments. Lowry also capitalizes words that identify people's positions in the community. For instance, Jonas's dad is a Nurturer, Jonas is a Twelve, the man who trains him is The Receiver, then The Giver.

Another way Lowry establishes her unfamiliar setting is by giving the reader a community in which people's lives are mapped out for them from birth to death. A baby is raised in the Nurturing Center. At the December ceremony it is Named and delivered to his or her new family unit. Each successive December that child moves up to the next age group and assumes that group's rights and responsibilities. At the Ceremony of Twelve the child will be assigned his or her lifelong job in the community. Eventually, an adult may apply to receive a spouse. Then the Committee of Elders monitors the couple for three years before allowing the spouses to apply for children. Once their children are grown, the spouses move into a group home, where they live with other Childless Adults. Eventually, when they are old enough, they go to live at the House of the Old, where they live out their final days, until they are released from the community.

Lowry also establishes the uniqueness—and eeriness—of her setting by showing that there is no privacy. There is always someone watching you, and someone listening to you. The reader sees that Jonas is being watched when the boy recalls an incident when he took an apple home from the recreation area and, later, hears this public announcement: "ATTENTION. THIS IS A REMINDER TO MALE ELEVENS THAT OBJECTS ARE NOT TO BE REMOVED FROM THE RECREATION AREA AND THAT SNACKS ARE TO BE EATEN, NOT HOARDED." The speakers in each home are not just for public announcements, they are for private listening. So when family members are required to share feelings and dreams with one another, they are also sharing them with whomever is listening in at the other end of that speaker. The only person who can turn off this speaker and listening device is The Receiver, or The Giver, as Jonas comes to call him.

Jonas's world is also a place that Lowry makes different by making it all the same. The Giver tells Jonas that before the community chose to go to Sameness there were hills, there was snow, there were colors. Many of the differences we take for granted in our world are missing from Jonas's.

Lowry uses all of the above and more to turn a world that is familiar—a world where children go to school, play catch, ride bikes, get annoyed at little sisters, snuggle stuffed animals, and coo at babies—into a world that is terribly strange.

Thinking about the setting
• Does *The Giver* take place anywhere that's familiar to you?
• When does *The Giver* take place?
• What first told you that *The Giver* takes place in a very different culture and time?

"'Giver,' Jonas suggested, 'you and I don't need to care about the rest of them.'

"The Giver looked at him with a questioning smile. Jonas hung his head. Of course they needed to care. It was the meaning of everything."

— *The Giver*

Connections

The importance of making connections is one of the major themes in *The Giver*. Lowry says that the book speaks to "the vital need for humans to be aware of their interdependence, not only with each other, but with the world and its environment."

When Jonas begins his training, The Giver says that he must transmit "the memories of the whole world" to Jonas. Because The Giver has all these memories, his life is much richer than the lives of other members of the community. He can see color, he can hear music, he can feel love. But he can also feel pain, and that is a great burden to him. When Jonas sees The Giver suffering, he wants to help him. "What is it that makes you suffer so much?" he asks. "If you gave some of it to me, maybe your pain would be less."

The Giver does give Jonas pain, and Jonas suffers from these memories, but not as much as if he had to bear them alone. He is glad that he can share them with The Giver, though he wishes the memories could be shared by the whole community. The Giver agrees. "The worst part of holding the memories is not the pain. It's the loneliness of it. Memories need to be shared."

The Giver and Jonas work out a plan to return the memories to the community. It means Jonas must leave and never come back. Although Jonas is sad to leave The Giver, and initially wants his friend to leave with him, he knows that The Giver must stay. He needs to help the others. As Jonas realizes, "Of course they needed to care. It was the meaning of everything."

Lowry feels her connectedness to others even when she's alone at her desk writing. "When I'm working in isolation, I feel I have a great bond with a world of people, of children, and adults who care about things, who feel the same way about things. That's what Jonas didn't have."

Choice

Choice—which Jonas had very little of—is another important theme in this book. Lowry says, "*The Giver* relates to me in probably the same way it relates to everybody—it is a reminder of the importance of the choices we make; also of the value of our freedom to make choices."

Jonas is made aware of the importance of choices we make when he looks back at the choices the community has made. He sees all that has been lost since the community decided to go to Sameness: snow, hills, sleds, color, and choice.

He truly regrets the loss of choice. "If everything's the same," he says, "then there aren't any choices! I want to wake up in the morning and *decide* things! A blue tunic, or a red one?"

Then The Giver points out that along with the freedom of choice comes the possibility of making the wrong choices. Jonas understands the community's reasoning behind taking away choice. He almost believes it. "We really have to protect people from wrong choices," he says. It's "much safer." But even as he speaks these words, he feels uneasy with them.

Freedom versus security

Loss of choice is loss of freedom, and another important theme in *The Giver* is freedom versus security. Lowry describes the perfect world she created in the book: "I tried to make Jonas's world seem familiar, comfortable, and safe, and I tried to seduce the reader. I seduced myself along the way. It did feel good, that world. I got rid of all the things I fear and dislike: all the violence, prejudice, poverty, and injustice; and I even threw in good manners as a way of life because I liked the idea of it. . . . It was very, very tempting to leave it at that. But I've never been a writer of fairy tales. And if I've learned anything . . . it is that we can't live in a walled world, in an 'only us, only now' world, where we are all the same and feel safe. We would have to sacrifice too much."

Jonas, in choosing to run away, comes to the same conclusion. He knows that if he gets caught, "he would very likely be killed. But," he thinks, "what did that matter? If he stayed, his life was no longer worth living."

Even when he and Gabe are cold and starving, and Jonas wonders if he made the right choice to run away, he can't help believing that he did. He knows that if he had stayed in the community, he would not be starving. But, "if he had stayed, he would have starved in other ways. He would have lived a life hungry for feelings, for color, for love."

Jonas was unwilling to give up all that. He was also unwilling to sacrifice his humanity—his ability to care for others—for the safety and security his community provided. He could not live in a place that would kill a baby because he did not sleep through the night.

Sameness versus diversity

One area where Jonas's community finds security is in Sameness, which leads to the theme of sameness versus diversity. On this subject, Lowry says, "I think that people are always more comfortable with familiar things. It is not easy to stand out, and that's why teenagers like to wear the same sneakers as other teenagers. The world of *The Giver* is a world where nobody has to take any risks. It's a very safe and comfortable world."

So much is the same in Jonas's world: He and his groupmates wear the same kind of clothes, they ride the same kind of bicycles, they have the same kind of family units. The streets are flat, the weather is unvarying, there is no color. Until he spends time with The Giver, Jonas is unaware of this Sameness. Once he learns of it, though, he is unhappy with it. He wants colors, he wants snow and hills and sleds. When The Giver explains that they had to let go of some things to gain control of others, Jonas says, "We shouldn't have!"

When Jonas runs away from his community, from Sameness, he finds a world of unexpected pleasures: "After a life of Sameness and predictability, he was awed by the surprises that lay beyond each curve of the road."

Individuality

In a community that values Sameness, there is no room for individuality, which is another theme in *The Giver*. In Jonas's community, being your own person is frowned upon. The Chief Elder says at the Ceremony of Twelve, "You Elevens have spent all your years till now learning to fit in, to standardize your behavior, to curb any impulse that might set you apart from the group." It is only in their Assignments that their differences are acknowledged and honored.

Children do not celebrate individual birthdays, they do not even know their actual birthdays; instead, they turn the next age with their groupmates at the December Ceremonies. When The Giver gives Jonas the memory of a birthday party, "with one child singled out and celebrated on his day," Jonas comes to understand "the joy of being an individual, special and unique and proud."

Honesty

Honesty is another theme in *The Giver*. When Jonas receives the rules and instructions that he must follow in his training, he is most disturbed by the final rule, "You may lie." He has been trained since he was a very young child never to lie. When he hears this, he wonders whether others, upon becoming Twelves, have been told, "You may lie." Do adults lie to him? He knows, given his rules and instructions, that he could ask adults—his parents, even—if they lie. "But," he thinks, "he would have no way of knowing if the answer he received were true."

He learns that his father has lied to him when he watches the tape of his father euthanizing the newborn twin. When talking about the "release" the night before, Jonas had asked his father about the procedure, had specifically asked if somebody else came to get the baby, somebody from Elsewhere, and his father had said yes, "That's right, Jonas-bonus." When Jonas sees that his father actually kills the baby, he is horrified. And he is angry.

"He *lied* to me," Jonas cries. The Giver tries to console Jonas, telling him that his father was just doing what he was told to do. "He knows nothing," he tells Jonas.

Jonas asks if The Giver lies to him, too. "I am empowered to lie," The Giver says. "But I have never lied to you." The Giver has made the choice to be honest.

Family

Another theme in this book is family. What makes a family? In *The Giver*, families are called family units. They do not start with a man and woman falling in love and deciding to start a family, families start with a man or a woman applying for a spouse. Then, once the committee matches them with one, the couple must prove their compatability for three years before they are allowed to apply for a child.

Children are not born in a family, they are born in a Birthing Center by Birthmothers. They are raised in a Nurturing Center until the December after their birth, at which time they are given to parents the committee has chosen from among the applicants. Each family unit is allowed one male and one female child.

When children are grown, the parents move out of the family dwelling to live with other Childless Adults. They are no longer part of their children's lives. There is no intergenerational connectedness. There are no grandparents.

Jonas does not miss grandparents, or know to miss them, until The Giver gives him his favorite memory, which involves several generations of people sitting around a Christmas tree opening gifts. He tells The Giver, "I can see that it wasn't a very practical way to live, with the Old right there in the same place, where maybe they wouldn't be well taken care of, the way they are now, and that we have a better-arranged way of doing things. But anyway, I was thinking, I mean feeling, actually, that it was kind of nice, then. And that I wish we could be that way, and that you could be my grandparent." Jonas sees—and wants—a family that is bound not just by duty and obligation, but by love.

Thinking about the themes

- What do *you* think is the most important theme in *The Giver*?
- How much would you be willing to give up to live in a safe and secure world? Would you give up as much as the people in Jonas's community?
- What are the good and bad things about Jonas's family?

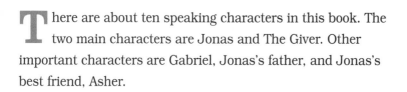

There are about ten speaking characters in this book. The two main characters are Jonas and The Giver. Other important characters are Gabriel, Jonas's father, and Jonas's best friend, Asher.

Here is a list of characters. Following that, there is a brief description of each of the main characters.

Jonas	a boy turning twelve
The Giver	the person who holds the memories of the world
Gabriel	a baby Jonas grows to love, called Gabe
Father	Jonas's father
Mother	Jonas's mother
Lily	Jonas's younger sister
Asher	Jonas's best friend
Fiona	Jonas's friend
Larissa	a woman in the House of the Old
Chief Elder	the leader of the community

Jonas: Jonas, the main character in the book, is an eleven-year-old boy on the verge of becoming an adult in his community. Jonas is an introspective boy who thinks a good deal about what is happening around him. He is also curious, considerate, observant, intelligent, and brave.

From the beginning, it is clear that Jonas spends a lot of time thinking. He struggles to find just the right word to describe his feelings regarding the upcoming Ceremony of Twelve. He wonders about the apple that seemed to have changed while he was playing catch with Asher. He thinks about dreams, replaying them in his head. He tries to imagine how things might be different for the whole community.

Jonas is also curious. He wants to experience everything, despite the pain it might cause him. He wants to know about Elsewhere. He asks his father and The Giver about release. He takes full advantage of being able to ask The Giver questions.

That Jonas is very observant is especially obvious during and after the Ceremony of Twelve. He notices the hush in the crowd when the Chief Elder skips over him while making the Assignments; he notices his groupmates trying not to make eye contact; he notices the worried look on the face of his group leader. And he notices how Asher and others seem to treat him differently after he is given his Assignment.

Because he is so observant, Jonas can see when people are uncomfortable or need help, and is considerate in offering it. When he first meets The Giver, and the man says of his memories, "I am so *weighted* with them," Jonas feels "a terrible concern for the man." And when The Giver is miserable with pain, Jonas asks him to share it. "If you gave some of it to me, maybe your pain would be less," he says. And, just as he is willing to take away the man's greatest pain, he is unwilling to take away his greatest pleasure. When The Giver offers to give

Jonas some music before he leaves, Jonas refuses. "No, Giver," he says. "I want you to keep that, to have with you, when I'm gone."

Jonas shows his intelligence in a number of ways. He realizes that if his instructions tell him he can lie, the adults around him may lie to him, and that he will never know if they do because they do not have to answer him truthfully. After learning of colors, and how they were done away with when the community went to Sameness, Jonas says, "We shouldn't have!" He even shows his intelligence when he and Gabe run away: He uses memories of snow to cool them off so they will avoid detection by the search planes' heat-seeking devices, and memories of warmth to keep from freezing to death.

Finally, Jonas is brave. He does not feel brave when the Chief Elder describes him as such at the Ceremony of Twelve, but he goes on to show that he is very brave indeed. He is brave when he volunteers to take painful memories from The Giver to ease his burden. And he is brave when he runs away with Gabe. He risks capture, and with it almost certain death, but he knows that he has no choice. He has to run away to find a real life for himself, and he has to run away to let Gabe live his life.

The Giver: The Giver is another major character in this book. He is the current Receiver of Memory, and he trains Jonas to be his replacement. This man, one of the Elders in the community, is old beyond his years. Holding the memories of the whole world, alone, has worn him down. "This job has aged me," he tells Jonas. Through the course of the book, we see him as a considerate, loving, wise, and kind man.

The Giver shows his consideration in the memories he gives Jonas. He tries for a long while to avoid giving the boy painful memories. When he finally realizes he must—that it is his job and that he must lighten his burden—he feels awful. He cannot look at Jonas after giving him the memory of war. "Forgive me," he says.

Jonas also learns the true meaning of love from The Giver, as he is a very loving man. The Giver's favorite memory, which he gives to Jonas—of an extended family seated around a Christmas tree exchanging gifts—is suffused with love. Later, when The Giver tells Jonas about Rosemary, he reminds the boy of that memory. He tells him that that was the feeling he had for Rosemary. "I loved her," he says. "I feel it for you, too."

The Giver is also wise. He knows that the community pays far too great a price for safety and security. "There are so many things I could tell them," The Giver tells Jonas about the Committee of Elders. "I wish they would change. But they don't want change. Life here is so orderly, so predictable—so painless. It's what they've chosen."

In his wisdom, and with Jonas's help, The Giver finally realizes that he must do something to bring about change. "Having you here with me over the past year has made me realize that things must change. For years I've felt they should, but it seemed so hopeless. Now for the first time I think there might be a way." And he works out a plan for Jonas to leave the community, thus returning all the memories back to the people.

The Giver is also kind. He could run away with Jonas—the boy repeatedly asks him to—but he refuses. He tells Jonas, "Remember how I helped you in the beginning, when the receiving of memories was new to you? . . . You needed me then. And now they will."

Gabriel: Gabriel is a baby that Jonas's father brings home at night for extra nurturing. He is small for his age and does not sleep through the night, so the Committee has labeled him Inadequate. If he does not grow and learn to sleep through the night, the Committee will release him.

We know very little about Gabe: He has pale eyes, he is able to receive memories, and he sleeps poorly. But he is still an important character in the book. Through him, Jonas learns to give as well as receive memories. Gabe, and his impending release, force Jonas to run away early, taking the baby with him. The baby also gives Jonas a reason for living, for continuing the journey when he is starved and exhausted and almost without hope. Gabe is "the one person left for him to love." He is also Jonas's link with, and hope for, the future.

Father: Jonas's father is another important character in *The Giver.* He is quiet, thoughtful, and playful with babies and children. He is the only adult in the story who we hear using nicknames: He calls his daughter Lily-billy, his son Jonas-bonus.

His most important role in the book may be to help show Jonas that all is not as it appears. Jonas's father loves newchildren and spends his days happily caring for them. Yet he releases—

kills—them when their presence would somehow disrupt the community. He releases a newborn twin who might cause confusion in the community. When Jonas watches his father release the newborn, he sees the sacrifice his community makes for orderliness; he sees the lies everyone—including his father—must tell to make it all seem right. When Jonas learns that his father has voted to release Gabriel, because the baby does not sleep through the night, he knows he must run away and take the baby with him.

Asher: Asher, another Eleven, is Jonas's best friend. He has a cheerful disposition and always talks too fast and mixes up words. He is someone everyone enjoys, because he is fun and makes a game out of everything. Once Jonas gets memories, he realizes that he loves Asher. He also realizes that without memories, Asher cannot love him back.

Thinking about the characters
• Who would you rather have for a friend, Jonas or Asher? Why?
• Do you think The Giver would be a good grandfather? Why or why not?
• What does Gabe represent at the end of this book?
• How can Jonas's father be so fond of children and still perform releases?

It's a winner!

The Giver has won many awards, the most prestigious of which
is the 1994 Newbery Medal. This award is given annually to the
author of "the most distinguished contribution to American
literature for children" published the preceding year. The
selection is made by fifteen librarians on the American Library
Association's Newbery Committee. Look at your copy of *The Giver*
and you may see the award, printed in gold on the cover.

Lowry had previously won the 1990 Newbery Medal for her
historical novel *Number the Stars.* She remembers when the
time was approaching for the Newbery to be announced for
1994: "People were predicting that *The Giver* would win. I didn't
want to be waiting by the phone. I went on a trip where no one
could reach me. I was in Antarctica when they made the
announcement." When her publisher finally managed to reach
her by radioing her ship, Lowry was so excited that she turned to
the woman next to her and said, "You've probably never heard of
this, but I just won the Newbery Medal." The woman had indeed
heard of the award—she was the former president of the
American Library Association!

Censored!

While *The Giver* is a popular book, it is also a controversial one. It ranked number eleven on the American Library Association's list of most frequently challenged books of the 1990s. A challenged book is one that a person or a group of people has tried to have removed from library shelves.

Why has *The Giver* been challenged? Some people say the book is too violent. They object to the passages regarding what is referred to in the book as "release": infanticide and euthanasia. Others complain about references to Jonas's "stirrings," the natural result of increased hormone production in the body. Parents with such complaints have managed to get the book banned from some school districts or to make it required that a student needs a parent's permission to read the book.

How does Lois Lowry feel about *The Giver* being such a frequently challenged book? "I think it's an honor I would prefer to forgo," she says. "It's a difficult situation." Lowry worries about the chilling effect such controversy can have on librarians and teachers, and what it means regarding whether or not the book will be read. "Even though they [librarians and teachers] may like a book and want to teach the book, they don't have time to deal with the bureaucracy that's required, and they're likely to choose a less controversial book."

The end?

Probably the biggest complaint Lowry gets from children about *The Giver* has to do with its ending.

"Many kids want a more specific ending to *The Giver*," she says. "Some write, or ask me when they see me, to spell it out exactly. And I don't do that . . . because *The Giver* is many things to many different people. People bring to it their own complicated sense of beliefs and hopes and dreams and all of that. I don't want to put my own feelings into it, my own beliefs, and ruin that for people who create their own endings in their minds."

Lowry says that the open-ended conclusion is the reason she won't write a sequel to this popular book. "In order to write a sequel, I would have to say: This is how it ended. Here they are and here's what's happening next. And that might be the wrong ending for many, many people who chose something different."

Thinking about what others think about The Giver

- Do you think that *The Giver* seems like an award-winning book? What other Newbery Medal–winning books have you read? How does *The Giver* compare?
- How does the subject of censorship relate to the theme of *The Giver*? What do you think the leaders in Jonas's community would say about censorship? What would Jonas and The Giver say?
- How do you imagine *The Giver* ends? Would you like to see the ending more spelled out? Why or why not?

Here are some important words used in *The Giver.* Understanding these words will make it easier to read the novel.

anguish a strong feeling of misery or distress

annex an extra building that is joined onto or placed near a main building

apprehensive worried and slightly afraid

buoyancy the ability to keep afloat

chastise to punish or criticize for wrongdoing

counsel advice

dejected sad and depressed

depth deepness

destination the place that a person or vehicle is traveling to

diminish to become smaller or weaker

disposition a person's general mood

exempted freed or excused from a certain duty or obligation

fugitives persons who are running away, especially from the authorities

integrity being honest and fair

interdependence dependency on one another

meticulous very careful and precise

monitored kept watch over

nurturer a person who tends to the needs of someone, especially a child

obsolete out-of-date and no longer used

ominous threatening; signaling trouble, danger, or disaster

petitioned made a formal request

phenomenon something very unusual and remarkable

precision accuracy or exactness

prestige honor or esteem

prohibited forbidden

regulated controlled or managed

relinquish to give up

restriction something that limits

rueful full of regret, remorse, or sorrow

scrupulously with extreme care about details

solace comfort or relief from sorrow or grief

solemn very serious; grave

standardize to make the same as everyone or everything else

stirrings exciting, strong feelings

summit the highest point; the top

tentatively with uncertainty

transgression a violation of a law or duty

transmit to send or pass something from one person or place to another

violation an act or instance of breaking a rule or law

yearning a strong wish for something

Lois Lowry delights in writing books for young people. "It's what I do best," she says, "and it's what I like doing best." She has written more than twenty-five books for children and young adults and won numerous awards—including the prestigious Newbery twice—for her work. How does she do it?

"It would be wonderful to be able to describe some ritualistic approach to writing fiction," Lowry says. "But the truth is so much more mundane. I sit at my desk every day. . . . I type words into my computer. I retype them, rearrange them, and delete them, and retype them again and again. . . . Then I look at the words I've written and rearrange them again. Eventually, somehow, a story is put together. There isn't anything magical. It's a lot of hard work, a lot of fun, and a lot of waiting for the words."

Though Lowry has to wait for the right words, she knows a good deal about the book she's going to write before she begins writing. "Books start in my head long before I start them on my computer," she says. "Before I ever sit down to write a book, I spend a lot of time going over it in my head."

When Lowry begins a book, she has "the main characters, the beginnings of the plot, and a sense of the theme. The secondary characters and the complications of the plot all come to me after I begin writing, and then I follow my imagination through the pages of the book. Parts of it take me by surprise when I'm writing."

Sometimes it's the endings that surprise her. "The characters create the ending," she says. "I only move the characters along and tell what they do. The decisions they make determine what the outcome will be."

As for theme, Lowry says, "My books have varied in content and style. Yet it seems to me that all of them deal, essentially, with the same general theme: the importance of human connections."

It takes Lowry about six months to write a book, and then a little additional time for rewriting. Once she has finished the book and reread it, she chooses a title. "I think a good title should be fairly short, easy to remember, easy to say, and should tell something about the book without revealing too much."

Then she sends the manuscript to her publisher. They usually ask for revisions, which, though Lowry might not like doing them, she does, because she knows revisions make the book better. Revisions usually take about a month, then the book is complete.

By the time one book is published, Lowry is well into writing her next one. Where does she get her ideas? "Ideas come from your imagination," Lowry says. "If you are a writer you are also an observant person. . . . And when you observe something, your imagination begins to play." If you are observant, she says, you will never run out of ideas. "I think ideas are there in the millions. The hard part is choosing which idea to focus on."

For aspiring writers

Lowry has two important pieces of advice for aspiring writers: Read and write.

"Read a lot. I mean really a LOT," Lowry says. "And when you're reading, think about how the author did things. How did the author create a character who is interesting? . . . How did the author create suspense?"

Lowry practices what she preaches. "Reading is the most productive thing for me," she says. "If I read brilliant paragraphs, I want to rush out and write brilliant paragraphs. . . . Whatever you read affects what you write."

And it's so important that you write. "I always tell children that they should write letters to their grandparents, and they groan when I say that," Lowry says. "But I don't mean it as a joke. The best way to write fiction is to write it as if you're telling a story to a friend. Getting into the habit of writing letters to friends and grandparents is a great way to practice writing fiction. The best fiction has that kind of intimate quality to it. And, if you're not in the habit of writing with that warmth and intimacy, then your fiction becomes stilted."

• **Character sketch:** Lowry knows her main characters intimately when she begins a book. She says that she knows "how they dress, behave, talk, react." You can get to know the characters in your stories in the same way. Think of a story you might like to write. Who are the main characters? Write a character sketch for each, telling how the character dresses, behaves in different situations, talks, and reacts to different things. Does your character have a nickname? What are her favorite—and least favorite—foods? What are his fears, likes, and dislikes? Include in the character sketch everything you can think of to help bring the character to life in your mind; this will help you bring your character to life on the page.

• **To be continued . . . :** Lowry is known for writing ambiguous, or unclear, endings to her books. She does this to allow "readers to create their own answer" to how the story ends. How do you think *The Giver* ends? What happens to Jonas and Gabe? What happens in the community? Write a page—or more—telling how you think the story ends.

• **Keep a journal:** When Lowry was young, she "endlessly scribbled stories and poems in notebooks." Do the same. Also, keep track of what happens in your life and in the lives of those around you, and how it makes you feel. You may use these notes, and the memories they evoke, one day. "Everything a writer experiences as a young person goes into the later writing in some form," Lowry says. "As writers all we have, really, is the memory of our own past combined with observation."

• **Observe:** Lowry says, "I think all writers are observers and so everywhere I go I am absorbing the details of that place." If you want to write you also need to observe. Make a point of doing as Lois Lowry does, and try to absorb the details of life around you. If you need help remembering what you see (smell, hear, taste, touch, and feel), keep a small notebook and pen with you and write down your observations.

• **Write a letter:** Follow Lowry's advice and become a better fiction writer by writing letters to family and friends. The best letters—like the best books—are those that tell great stories. Writing down your real-life stories in a way that will interest friends and relatives will make you a better storyteller when it comes to writing fiction. It will also make you more popular with friends and relatives, as everyone enjoys a good letter!

- **Make a memory book:** Memories are an important part of *The Giver* because they are an important part of life. Make a memory book to help record some of your important memories. Use a loose-leaf notebook or a book of your own making; whichever you use, be sure to allow room to add more memory pages as additional memories come to you. Begin by making a list of people, places, and events that have been important in your life. Look at each item on the list and see what memory or memories arise in your mind. Then, think of ways to record these memories. You might write a poem, a sentence, a paragraph, even a story; you might draw or paint a picture, or use a photograph you already have. Transfer these memories to your book, just as The Giver transfers memories to Jonas. Unlike The Giver, however, you'll still have the memories in your head; your book will just be a way to help you remember them, as well as a way for you to share your memories with others.

- **Get a library card!:** If you don't already have a library card, get one—and use it. Librarians will help you find whatever kind of book you're looking for—funny, sad, scary—and even make some good suggestions if you tell them what kinds of books you like.

- **Picture this cover!:** Lois Lowry is an accomplished photographer as well as a wonderful writer; she took the two photos on the cover of *The Giver*. If you have access to a camera, take a photograph of your own that you think would be a good cover for this book. Illustrate your cover if you don't have a camera. In either case, as you do your cover remember to think about what you want to say with your image, what you want to tell the reader about the book. Remember, too, that your goal should be to make a person want to pick up the book and read it.

• **Bike or hike:** In Jonas's community, the primary means of transportation was bicycle. Only when the citizens visited other communities, which was rare, did they travel by car or bus. Think about how limited your range of movement would be if you could only travel on foot or by bicycle. If possible, spend a day in which you do not get in a car or on a bus or train. See if you can get your family to go along with you in this experiment. At the end of the day, talk about how your life would be different if you always had such restrictions on how you could travel.

• **Winning ways:** Lois Lowry won the 1994 Newbery Medal for *The Giver*. Read one or two other Newbery-winning books and think about what it takes to be a winner. Some recent Newbery Medal–winning books are:

Crispin: The Cross of Lead by Avi (2003)
A Single Shard by Linda Sue Park (2002)
A Year Down Yonder by Richard Peck (2001)
Bud, Not Buddy by Christopher Paul Curtis (2000)
Holes by Louis Sachar (1999)
Out of the Dust by Karen Hesse (1998)
The View from Saturday by E. L. Konigsburg (1997)

The Midwife's Apprentice by Karen Cushman (1996)
Walk Two Moons by Sharon Creech (1995)
Missing May by Cynthia Rylant (1993)

• **What's in a name?:** Names are very important in *The Giver*. There is a great deal of thought put into naming each newchild. Think about your name. Who chose it? Why was it given to you? Does it have special meaning in your family? You might want to look up its meaning in a book of names. Then, think about this: If you could choose a different name for yourself, what would it be? Why?

• **Become a Receiver of Memory:** Jonas was chosen to become the Receiver of Memory in his community. You can become a Receiver, too, simply by interviewing an elderly friend or relative about his or her past. You might want to find out what it was like to be a child during previous generations. What games did children play then? What did they wear? What did they eat? What was school like? What kind of chores did they do? Did they watch television? What about movies? What were the most popular names? You might want to take notes or tape-record your interview, so that later you can write it all down and share these memories again with your "Giver."

• **Visit the "old":** While we don't have a "House of the Old" where all the elderly go, as Jonas does in his community, we do have many nursing homes where a large number of elderly people live. Many of these people are lonely and have few visitors. You might like to ask an adult family member to arrange for you to visit a nursing home, once, or on a regular basis. In addition to bringing joy into other people's lives, you might also hear some wonderful memories from way back!

- **What is love?:** When Jonas asks his parents if they love him, they tell him that it's inappropriate to use a word like "love," that the word is "so meaningless that it's become almost obsolete." Think of someone you love, and find a way—a kind act, a poem, a card—to show that you love them.

- **Color my world:** Research color and light. The Howard Hughes Medical Institute has a Web site dedicated to the subject: www.hhmi.org/senses/b110.html.

- **Words, words, words:** Precision of language is very important in Jonas's world. His best friend, Asher, has gotten into trouble for repeatedly mixing up words, using *distraught* for *distracted*, *boyishness* for *buoyancy*, *smack* for *snack*, and *expertness* for *expertise*. Make a list of pairs of words that might easily be confused. Then, play a game with friends or family members in which you use the wrong word of the pair in a sentence and you see if they can identify the incorrect word, then think of the correct one.

- **Don't forget ...:** You can learn more about memory at the Exploratorium's online Memory Exhibition. The Web site is: www.exploratorium.edu/memory/index.html.

Other novels by Lois Lowry

Autumn Street (1979)

Gathering Blue (2000)

Number the Stars (1989)

Rabble Starkey (1987)

Stay! Keeper's Story (1997)

A Summer to Die (1977)

Taking Care of Terrific (1983)

Us and Uncle Fraud (1984)

Series by Lois Lowry

Anastasia series (*Anastasia Krupnik, Anastasia Again!*)

Sam series (*All About Sam, Attaboy, Sam!*)

Caroline and P. J. Tate series (*The One Hundredth Thing About Caroline, Switcharound*)

Autobiography by Lois Lowry

Looking Back (1998)

Science fiction and fantasy

Among the Hidden and *Among the Imposters* by Margaret Peterson Haddix

Coraline by Neil Gaiman

The Hermit Thrush Sings by Susan Butler

The Moorchild by Eloise McGraw

Off the Road by Nina Bawden

The Phantom Tollbooth by Norton Juster

Tuck Everlasting by Natalie Babbitt

Under the Cat's Eye by Gillian Rubinstein

The White Mountains trilogy by John Christopher

A Wrinkle in Time by Madeleine L'Engle

Books

Lowry, Lois. *The Giver.* New York: Houghton Mifflin Co., 1993.

Lowry, Lois. *Looking Back.* New York: Houghton Mifflin Co., 1998.

Newspapers and magazines

The Horn Book Magazine, July/August 1990, Volume 66, Issue 4, pp. 412–424.

The Horn Book Magazine, July/August 1993, Volume 69, Issue 4, p. 392.

The Horn Book Magazine, November/December 1993, Volume 69, Issue 6, pp. 717–720.

The Horn Book Magazine, July/August 1994, Volume 70, Issue 4, pp. 414–426.

The Reading Teacher, December 1994/January 1995, Volume 48, Number 4, pp. 308–309.

Web sites

Bookpage interview with Lois Lowry:
wildes.home.mindspring.com/OUAL/int/lowrylois.html

BookSense interview with Lois Lowry:
www.booksense.com/people/archive/lowry.jsp

CNN online article, "Book Challenges Drop, but Librarians, Writers, Remain Wary":
www.cnn.com/2000/books/news/09/26/banned.books/

The Internet Public Library:

www.ipl.org/youth/AskAuthor/Lowry.html

Lois Lowry's Web site:

www.loislowry.com

Random House, "A Message from the Author":

www.randomhouse.com/teachers/authors/lowr.html

Scholastic, Lois Lowry biography and interview:

www2.scholastic.com/teachers/authorsandbooks/
authorstudies/authorstudies.jhtml